D1568607

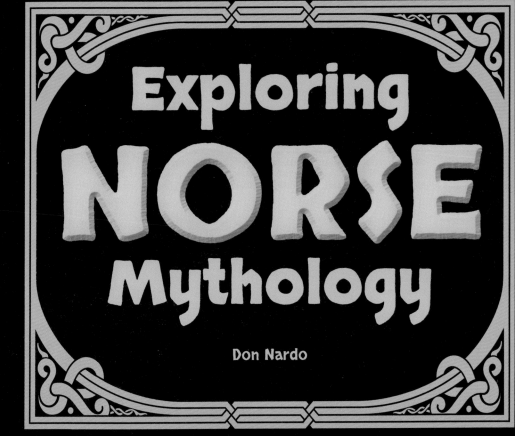

Exploring
NORSE
Mythology

Don Nardo

ReferencePoint
Press

San Diego, CA

About the Author

Classical historian and award-winning author Don Nardo has written numerous acclaimed volumes about ancient civilizations and peoples. They include more than four dozen overviews of the mythologies of the Sumerians, Babylonians, Egyptians, Greeks, Romans, Persians, Celts, Chinese, Aztecs, Hindus, Native Americans, and others. Nardo, who also composes and arranges orchestral music, lives with his wife, Christine, in Massachusetts.

For more information, contact:
ReferencePoint Press, Inc.
PO Box 27779
San Diego, CA 92198
www.ReferencePointPress.com

Picture Credits:
Cover: Barandash Karandashich/Shutterstock
  6: Maury Aaseng
10: Chronicle/Alamy Stock Photo
13: Charles Walker Collection/Alamy Stock Photo
14: Ivy Close Images/Alamy Stock Photo
20: picture-alliance/Judaica-Samml/Newscom
23: © Ashmolean Museum/Bridgeman Images
25: Universal History Archive/UIG/Bridgeman
      Images
30: PRISMA ARCHIVO/Alamy Stock Photo
32: Artokoloro/Alamy Stock Photo
35: Pictures Now/Alamy Stock Photo
40: New Line Cinema/Photofest
43: Glasshouse Images/Alamy Stock Photo
46: Skimage/Alamy Stock Photo
49: Uber Bilder/Alamy Stock Photo
50: Chronicle/Alamy Stock Photo
54: British Library/Alamy Stock Photo

LIBRARY OF CONGRESS CATALOGING-IN-PUBLICATION DATA

Names: Nardo, Don, 1947- author.
Title: Exploring Norse mythology / by Don Nardo.
Description: San Diego, CA : ReferencePoint Press, Inc., 2023. | Includes
   bibliographical references and index.
Identifiers: LCCN 2022048736 (print) | LCCN 2022048737 (ebook) | ISBN
   9781678205720 (library binding) | ISBN 9781678205737 (ebook)
Subjects: LCSH: Mythology, Norse--Juvenile literature.
Classification: LCC BL860 .N26 2023 (print) | LCC BL860 (ebook) | DDC
   398.209368--dc23/eng 20230126
LC record available at https://lccn.loc.gov/2022048736
LC ebook record available at https://lccn.loc.gov/2022048737

CONTENTS

Eager Achievers in an Enchanted World

Apparently, few if any in Valhalla pitied poor Saehrimnir. Valhalla was a fabled great hall in the afterlife where some Norse heroes who had died in battle dined and socialized with the chief Norse god, Odin. And Saehrimnir was a large, boar-like creature on whose meat those warriors repeatedly feasted. Each afternoon, Andhrimnir, Odin's official chef, removed the best cuts of Saehrimnir's flesh from his plump body and cooked them with a mix of tasty spices in a spacious cauldron. Odin's servants then distributed the meat to the gathered warriors in the vast, noisy, jovial hall.

But how was it possible for the feasters to continue consuming Saehrimnir's flesh night after night, month after month, and year after year? The answer is exceedingly strange but perfectly logical. In some unexplainable, magical way, each morning the creature returned to life, and its flesh rapidly grew back. In that way, Saehrimnir was doomed to go through the same agonizing procedure again and again as the revelers in Valhalla feasted.

Teeming with Supernatural Entities

The Norse, frequently called the Vikings, were the hardy, often warlike inhabitants of Scandinavia, the northern European region including Norway, Sweden, Denmark, and some nearby European regions during the mid-to-late medieval era. Saehrimnir's sad, strange story illustrates two of the most important aspects of the collected myths of these people. The first of those two crucial aspects of Norse people's beliefs was the way they envisioned their world and its underpinnings. In their view, that universe was enchanted, or infused with divine and magical presences and forces, both visible and invisible. On the one hand, it was thought that daily life was directed or influenced by either an invisible force—fate—or the will of various gods. Being divine, the latter could be visible or invisible depending on their mood or purpose as they intervened in human affairs.

On the other hand, the Norse believed that nature was teeming with diverse forms of non-divine supernatural entities that could and sometimes did affect people's lives. These beings included giants, dragons, dwarfs, elves, ghosts, so-called land spirits who dwelled inside rocks, and angel-like female spirits called Valkyries. Each of these mystical races was well described. For example, noted scholar William R. Short writes that dwarfs are "wise and skilled in crafts. [Dwarfs] made the treasures of the gods . . . and they are the repository of secret wisdom. They live among the rocks away from light, because sunlight causes them to turn to stone. There is no evidence that the [dwarfs] were worshipped, but men were wary of them and took care not to offend them."[1] Fear or awe of such creatures affected people's beliefs and behaviors.

dwarfs
Creatures who were skilled at crafts and possessed hidden knowledge

land spirits
Spirits that lived inside rocks and ensured the prosperity of farmland

Origins of Norse Mythology

Deeds That Would Be Remembered

The second important aspect of Norse mythology illustrated by Saehrimnir's tale involves those who ate of his flesh each evening. The spirits of deceased warriors, along with selected gods whom Odin invited to dine, were among the leading and most accomplished figures of the Norse mythological world. Regarding the human fighters who gave their lives in battle, nearly all of them had grown up in the cold, often bleak environment of the Norse lands. There, farming could be difficult, and for most families, merely surviving from year to year could be an unsung struggle.

Yet the many men who chose a warrior's life were both fearless and determined to accomplish noteworthy deeds. They were therefore the principal achievers of the magic-laced world of Norse life and myths. Norse scholar Daniel McCoy explains that they

> didn't sugarcoat the sordidness, strife, and unfairness of earthly life, but instead attempted to master it through the accomplishment of great deeds for the benefit of oneself and one's people. A life full of such deeds was one of eager achievement and for many of the Norse, that was "the good life." What sort of deeds? Ones that would leave some sort of lasting mark on the world. Or put another way, deeds that would be hopefully remembered.[2]

In Norse society in general, therefore, a male's ultimate measure—what he would be remembered for—was not humdrum obedience to authority or social rules. Rather, the measure of a warrior was the level of achievement he attained through his courage and fighting skills. A surviving early Norse poem captures this vital principle embraced by those long-ago eager achievers in an enchanted world: "Wealth will pass; men will pass; you, too, likewise, will pass. One thing alone will never pass—the fame of one who has earned it."[3]

A Tree So Vast: The Mythical Norse World

Sol, also called Sunna, warily glanced out at the dark, bare-ly discernible plain that stretched to the horizon in front of her. It was not the darkness that disturbed and at times frightened her. After all, as the Norse sun goddess, in a few minutes she would mount her horse-drawn chariot, which would instantly give off a brilliant yellow-white glow as she touched it. That lovely radiance would light up the dark mountains and valleys below, and as she traversed the sky, she would bring sunlight to the cities, farms, forests, lakes, rivers, and other sectors of the world below. Ever since the creator gods had given her this important task, she had completed it without fail day after day, year after year, and century after century.

Sol's strong sense of duty was not the only factor that motivated her to drive across the sky each day, however. The other incentive—which was also the thing she feared the most—was the fierce, bloodthirsty wolf named Skoll.

This beast stalked her, at first hiding in the predawn shadows and then leaping upward in an attempt to seize her in its powerful jaws. Each day Skoll pursued Sol across the heavens, until it, like she, needed to stop and rest up for the next day's chase.

Even during her flight, the glowing goddess sometimes thought about her brother, the moon god Mani. He, too, was chased by a wolf, in his case across the night sky. In some ways they were both better off when they were young, she occasionally mused. In those days, she recalled, shortly after the creator gods had made them, they were in a state of infantile confusion, because they did not yet know what their place and purpose was. A thirteenth-century Norse literary work describes that confused state:

> The sun from the south, the moon's companion,
> her right hand cast about the heavenly horses.
> The sun knew not where she a dwelling had,
> the moon knew not what power he possessed,
> the stars knew not where they had a station.[4]

Although Sol eventually came to learn her purpose well, she did not yet know what lay in the future for her. Sadly, she was destined to lose the race she currently ran. The vicious Skoll would ultimately catch and devour her. Yet there was hope for future generations that survived. Sol had given birth to a daughter, whom she named Sol after herself. And following the mother's demise, the younger goddess was fated to assume the critical duty of driving the shining chariot across the sky, this time with no deadly creatures pursuing.

The Aesir and the Creation

The incredibly vast and complex world that Sol, Mani, and the younger Sol looked down upon and illuminated was unique among the visions of the universe compiled by the peoples of the past. It was neither a flat disk nor a sphere nor a landscape lying atop the back of a huge beast, as others have envisioned.

Instead, in the Vikings' worldview, people, animals, plants, mountains, seas, and other elements of nature existed within an unimaginably immense tree. The Norse name for it was Yggdrasil, but later generations of Europeans called it the World Tree. "Its branches reached the sky and spread over the earth," wrote the late scholar of Norse lore Magnus Magnusson. "At its base lay the Spring or Well of Fate, the source of all wisdom, tended by the three Norns [foreseers of fate, who could see] the destiny of all living creatures."[5]

Yggdrasil, known to later Europeans as the World Tree, encompasses the spiritual realms which made up the Vikings' understanding of the universe.

The way the Norse thought that this enormous tree came into existence was no less fascinating. They believed that well before the sky, mountains, forests, oceans, and other natural realms formed, three places—all equally foreboding and scary—existed. On one side was a mass of blazing fire called Muspelheim; on the other side loomed an extensive expanse of solid ice—Niflheim; and in the center between them lay a dark, featureless void called Ginnungagap. Occasionally, licks of flame reached across the gap and melted a bit of the ice; and in that way small droplets formed and floated around in Ginnungagap. These warm liquid globules eventually took on living properties and grew into a monstrous primeval creature known as Ymir.

And from the sweat of Ymir's foul-smelling armpits sprang an array of new creatures. Most were dim-witted giants of varied shapes who lived and died, making way for still more. But one, known as Buri, had godlike powers, including intelligence and great longevity. After mating with one of the giants, Buri had a son named Bor, who fathered the first of two races of gods.

Bor had three sons—Odin, Vili, and Ve. Of the three, Odin was by far the smartest, and he correctly foresaw that the future belonged to the beings in his family line. He, his kin, and their descendants formed the main race of gods—the Aesir. Acting decisively, Odin and his brothers killed Ymir, disassembled its huge body, and used the parts to create the World Tree. They also took note of two physically beautiful children of one of the giants Ymir had spawned—Sol and Mani. Welcoming them into the Aesir group, Odin assigned them the tasks of providing daily sunlight and nightly moonlight.

During this eventful round of creation, Odin and his brothers also fashioned a completely new race of creatures called humans. While walking along a beach, the three deities noticed two pieces of driftwood that were shaped almost exactly like their own bodies, with a head, two arms, and two legs. On a whim, Odin breathed life into the two

Aesir

The main race of Norse gods, headed by Odin

11

How Do We Know About Norse Myths?

In 1643 someone found a very old book sitting in a rustic, crumbling farmhouse in rural Iceland. That person turned the book over to a local bishop, who in turn gave it to the king of Denmark. The work is a collection of poems known as the *Poetic Edda* or *Elder Edda*. Scholars estimate that it was written sometime between 1270 and 1300 CE. The scribe who collected the poems remains unknown, but the *Poetic Edda* stands as the single most detailed account of old Norse myths found to date. Among the more than thirty poems composing the work are "The Wise Woman's Prophecy," "The Sayings of the High One," and "The Lay of Thrym." Supplementing the knowledge of Norse mythology contained in the *Poetic Edda* is the *Prose Edda*, also frequently called the *Younger Edda*. Its author was an Icelandic poet, historian, and chieftain, Snorri Sturluson, who flourished in the early 1200s. Extra pieces of information about the Norse gods and heroes and their stories appear in a history of Denmark penned in the 1100s by the Danish scholar Saxo Grammaticus and in a series of historical texts loosely called the Norse Sagas, which date to the 1200s and 1300s.

wooden forms, and Vili and Ve gave them the ability to see, hear, and talk. The three gods also presented the couple with suitable clothes and named the male one Ask and his female companion Embla. Finally, Odin carved out a new realm—Midgard—in the World Tree and made it humanity's homeland.

Realms of the World Tree

As the World Tree continued to grow under Odin's guidance, many other sections and realms besides the human domain, Midgard, sprang into existence. Perhaps the most exalted and impressive was Asgard, a mighty kingdom set aside only for the divine Aesir. In its midst were not only splendid dwellings for the various deities but also a massive, gold-lined, heavenly hall known as Valhalla. There, over time, Odin would come to welcome the souls of half of the brave Midgard warriors who had died fighting in battle. Those former human combatants not only dined and caroused with Odin, they also pledged to support and fight for him if and when he might need them in the future.

The souls of the other half of the battle-slain human heroes ended up in another section of Asgard called Folkvangr. That smaller realm was presided over by Freya, the multifaceted goddess of love, the fertility of the soil, sex, and war. She wore a magnificent cloak, called Valhamr, made up of falcon feathers and drove a chariot drawn by two large cats.

If Freya, Odin, or another god wanted to leave Asgard and travel to other parts of the World Tree—maybe Nidavellir, homeland of

The Norse war god Odin stands triumphantly upon a cliff, adorned in gold and carrying his favored weapons. Odin is often associated with wisdom, creation, and power.

the dwarfs, or Alfheim, realm of the elves—several roads and tunnels could be employed. But if a god desired to go to Midgard, or a human from Midgard sought to visit Asgard, there was only one option: to cross Bifrost, the rainbow bridge. As the nickname suggests, it was a multicolored arc that stretched between the two realms. Near the top of Bifrost was a cliff containing a cave, inside of which dwelled a member of the Aesir named Heimdall. His job was to eternally guard the bridge, and Asgard itself, from enemies or other intruders.

Meanwhile, located within the trunk of the universal tree—seen as underground by the world's inhabitants—was the underworld,

Bifrost

The rainbow bridge connecting Midgard to Asgard

Freya, the Norse goddess of love and war, is depicted in this illustration flying on a golden, cat-drawn chariot through a windy sky. She rules over Folkvangr, one of the mythical halls for fallen warriors.

or Hel, ruled by a goddess with that same name. The modern word *hell* derives from it. However, as Daniel McCoy explains,

> apart from the fact that Hel and Hell are both realms of the dead located beneath the ground, the two concepts have nothing in common. . . . [To the Norse] where one goes after death isn't any kind of reward for moral behavior or pious belief, or punishment for immoral behavior or impious belief. . . . The dead in Hel spend their time doing the same kinds of things that Viking Age men and women did: eating, drinking, fighting, sleeping, and so forth. It wasn't a place of eternal bliss or torment as much as it was simply a continuation of life somewhere else.[6]

The Gods in Their Niches

Still another sector of the World Tree was Vanaheimr, home of the Vanir, the collective name of a second race of Norse gods, though not as powerful as the Aesir. Associated in early Viking times with wisdom, soil fertility, and the skill of foretelling the future, at some point the Vanir challenged the Aesir to a fight and lost. Thereafter the defeated deities accepted their inferior status to the Aesir; some Vanir intermarried with Aesir, while others kept to themselves in Vanaheimr.

Although all the regions of the great World Tree had their purposes and were integral to the workings of the universe, two of those realms mattered the most to the Norse; Midgard and Asgard. This is understandable, considering that the relationship between the Norse and their gods defined their worldview. Their beliefs dictated that a separate god oversaw each aspect of the natural world. And the mystical deities supposedly kept a close eye on human behavior and affairs, so it made sense for people to pray to the gods to influence the outcomes of events, from prosperous harvests to victory in battle to good luck in business.

How the Norse Worshipped the Gods

Only some of the ways in which the Norse worshipped their gods are known today. This is largely because in the years after most Vikings converted to Christianity, church officials hid the existing writings that described Scandinavian pagan rituals. Eventually, church leaders had the bulk of those documents destroyed. Fortunately for the modern world, archaeologists have been able to piece together an approximate overview of that pagan worship. It appears that most rituals were held in barns owned by individual Vikings. A few ceremonies took place in locations in the countryside deemed sacred. Meeting in those spots, worshippers carved wooden figures of gods and prayed to them. They made sacrifices, or offerings to the gods. Most common was to sacrifice cattle, goats, and other animals, believing this appeased the gods. A variation was to hang the head, or sometimes the entire body, of an animal above the door of one's home. Also, wearing or carrying an amulet, a carved object thought to possess magical properties, supposedly pleased the gods. To further win favors with the gods and thereby make it to the afterlife, many Norse routinely buried amulets, the remains of sacrificed animals, weapons, and foodstuffs with the dead.

As the leading god and chief creator of humanity, Odin received more prayers than any other deity. But that does not mean that the favor of the other gods was not routinely sought. Odin's wife, Frigg, for instance, goddess of motherhood, womanly love, and fate, was widely popular. No less so was Odin's son Thor, god of thunder and battle, to whom Norsemen appealed when strength was needed or victory sought. In the Norse myths, according to the late scholar of Viking lore H.R.E. Davidson,

> Thor appears as a burly, red-headed man, immensely strong, with a huge appetite, blazing eyes, and a beard, full of enormous vitality and power. He could increase his strength by wearing a special belt of might. Other prize possessions of his were his great gloves, enabling him to grasp and shatter rocks, the chariot drawn by goats which took him across the sky, and his hammer. This last was regarded as the greatest of all the treasures of Asgard, for Thor and his hammer formed a protection against the giants and the monsters, the enemies of gods and men.[7]

In addition to Odin, Frigg, Freya, Heimdall, Hel, and Thor, other prominent Norse gods were Odin's and Frigg's son Baldr, god of fairness and peace; Tyr, god of war; Foresti, god of justice; Eir, goddess of healing; Freyr, god of prosperity (and Freya's brother); Odin's son Vali, god of revenge; and Loki, the so-called trickster, who sometimes supported and other times opposed the other gods.

The stories of these deities and their unique world "have been retold to different audiences in different ways repeatedly over the years," states Beth Daley of the Conversation, an online collection of articles written by academics and other experts. "But what makes the Norse myths so irresistible?" she asks. Her answer is: "The distinctive, human characterization of the Norse gods . . . and their grandly tragic, absurdly comic, strangely moving tales."[8]

Thor's Hammer and Odin's Wisdom: Divine Quests

One day in the dim past, Odin, leader of the Norse gods, set out on a special quest. Frequently referred to with the utmost respect as the "All-Father," he was a war god, a controller of storms, and a master of magic. Tall, gaunt, and almost always bearing a serious expression, he sported a long white beard and most often wore a dark cloak and carried a spear.

In addition to ruling Asgard, the realm of the gods, Odin devoted as much time as he could to finding secret forms of knowledge and wisdom. More specifically, he was nearly obsessed with seeking out things that were connected in various ways with thinking, knowing, and creating. For his special quest, for example, he wanted to discover the innermost workings of nature. There was only one way to acquire that wisdom; he would have to pay a visit to a highly secretive supernatural being named Mimir, who was said to oversee a magical spring called Mímisbrunnr, or "Mimir's Well." Its murky, mysterious waters supposedly contained vast knowledge, which Mimir himself had acquired through drinking the precious liquid.

Eager to partake of that concealed information, Odin approached the well—an irregularly shaped, dark-colored pool shaded by a grove of tall trees. On a flat rock on the far side of the pool sat an extremely old man whose silvery beard was even longer than the All-Father's. This, Odin reasoned, had to be the legendary Mimir.

Mímisbrunnr (Mimir's well)

A magical pool of water that supposedly contained a vast amount of knowledge

Having heard that no one could taste the well's water without obtaining Mimir's express permission, Odin introduced himself, to which the other replied that he was already aware of who stood before him. When the god requested permission to drink, Mimir issued a grim warning. Anyone who drank from the pool was required to pay a toll—one involving a serious personal sacrifice. In Odin's case, Mimir explained, that hefty fee consisted of giving up one of his own eyes.

The All-Father raised an eyebrow and thought it over. It was a steep price indeed, he finally told Mimir, but he was willing to pay it. Wasting no time, Odin removed a knife from his belt, carefully yet swiftly employed the blade to scoop out his right eye, and tossed the now sightless orb into dark Mímisbrunnr. The well's overlord then kept his side of the ghastly bargain by filling a drinking horn with water from the pool and giving it to the now one-eyed deity. Odin took a sip, and thanks to the enormous collection of facts that suddenly rushed into his mind, he became by far the wisest of the Norse gods.

Searching for Power and Secret Wisdom

The search for secrets from Mimir's well is not the only legendary quest contained in the colorful annals of Norse mythology. Odin himself went on other such voyages of discovery, and other Norse gods, including Odin's son Thor, went on journeys that involved intrigue, adventure, or both. All those divine quests had something in common. In each case, the searcher looked for an object or arcane knowledge that would endow its possessor with great power of one kind or another.

Several historians have suggested that this fascination with vast, usually superhuman powers reflected the more mundane, often difficult realities of Norse life. Living in the mostly cold, mountainous wilderness areas of northern Europe was challenging, even for the few in society with wealth and high position. And most people accepted that they were largely powerless to control nature or change whatever fate might have in store for them. In such conditions, experts theorize, hearing and repeating stories about valiant quests for power and nature's secrets was almost certainly comforting and entertaining. In H.R.E. Davidson's words, such myths constitute "a vigorous, heroic comment on life, life as [people] found it in hard and inhospitable lands."[9]

Particularly in Odin's quests, in which he sought hidden knowledge, could the Vikings find hope that nature contained worthwhile, inspiring elements beyond what their senses perceived. "Odin represented," Davidson says, "the inspiration granted to the warrior and the poet and the secret wisdom won by commu-

In this illustration, Odin (right) and Mimir discuss the costly offering of the Norse god's right eye in exchange for a drink from the Mímisbrunnr.

nication with the dead . . . [and the power] to reach out beyond this harsh and limited world."[10]

The Magic of the Runes

One way that Odin reached out to unseen realms was by using potent magical powers. Some, of course, he possessed simply by virtue of being divine. But he was always looking for more powerful magic. And he became famous for launching a dramatic quest to learn the magical secrets of the pictographic alphabet called runes. These, Daniel McCoy writes,

> are the written letters that were used by the Norse and other Germanic peoples before the adoption of the Latin alphabet in the later Middle Ages. . . . The runes are symbols of some of the most powerful forces in the cosmos. . . . [They] allow one to access, interact with, and influence the world-shaping forces they symbolize. Thus, when Odin sought the runes, he . . . was uncovering an extraordinarily potent system of magic.[11]

Odin understood that acquiring the secrets held within this alphabet would not be easy. Indeed, he suspected that, like the successful acquisition of Mimir's secret wisdom, some sort of personal sacrifice would likely be necessary. In this regard, he was right. He knew that the runes existed mainly in the realm of the Norns, the three goddesses who had the ability to see some aspects of the future. Their desolate land lay far below Asgard and Midgard, in the very roots of the World Tree. Swiftly traveling downward to a spot directly above the Norns' domain, Odin tied himself to a tree branch and jabbed his spear into his side. As his blood slowly but steadily seeped out, he waited. He had reasoned that the Norns would not give up the rune secrets to anyone unless that person was willing to pay for the privilege by undergoing considerable suffering. Hence, he hung there, bleeding, without food or drink, for nine days, waiting for the Norns to acknowledge his presence.

Thor's Background and Personal Life

Thor, who wielded his mighty hammer to protect the gods and humans from their enemies, was the son of Odin, leader of the Norse gods. Thor's mother was Jord, a giantess, which made him half giant. Nevertheless, except for his mother, he hated all giants. In young adulthood, Thor married Sif, one of the several Norse deities associated with fertility. The two had a daughter named Thudr. Also, as a young man, Thor built a house in Asgard, a building he called Bilskirnir. It was the largest of all the personal residences of the Norse gods, supposedly featuring 540 rooms. Among the many bedchambers in that mansion were the two where Thor's faithful servants, Thialfi and Roskva, slept. Male and female twins, the two accompanied their divine master almost everywhere. Thor and his two servants often rode together in the god's chariot, which was drawn by two huge goats—Tanngrisnir and Tanngnjostr. To the amazement of many Norse, that god regularly cooked and ate the goats but late at night used his magical hammer to resurrect them.

Finally, in the morning of the tenth day, those elusive beings showed themselves. They decided that the All-Father had suffered enough and revealed the runes to him. The realization of the shapes and meanings of those symbols invigorated his damaged body and provided him with three new magical powers—the abilities to heal the sick, speak to the dead, and peer partway into the future.

The Gift of Poetry

Still another quest that the leader of the gods pursued was his search for the ability to create inspiring speech and written words, sometimes called the "gift of poetry." Although he knew that the powers of wisdom and magic were vital to have, he felt that the power of creative expression was no less crucial. To acquire that new power, Odin was told, he would need to drink a bit of a special brew known as the Mead of Poetry.

The only place in the known world where that peculiar drink existed was in a keg stored in a cave in Jotunheim, the land

Jotunheim

The realm of the giants located within the World Tree

of the giants. This presented a challenge because most of those huge beings hated the gods, including Odin. Nevertheless, he was not afraid and journeyed to Jotunheim on his trusty eight-legged flying horse, Sleipnir. There, he dug a tunnel through the side of the mountain containing the cave holding the keg. Next, he utilized his ability to mimic any creature's form by taking the shape of a serpent. That allowed him to slither through the tunnel until he reached the cave and the keg of mead.

Odin drank the mead, crawled back out of the cave, and returned to Asgard, now having the ability to speak and write with amazing skill, a talent he passed on to others. Compared to the gods in many other mythologies, he was remarkably unselfish and became even more so each time he gained new knowledge. So, in time, little by little, he shared most of the secrets he had acquired with human beings. The Norse came to call them "Odin's gifts to humanity."

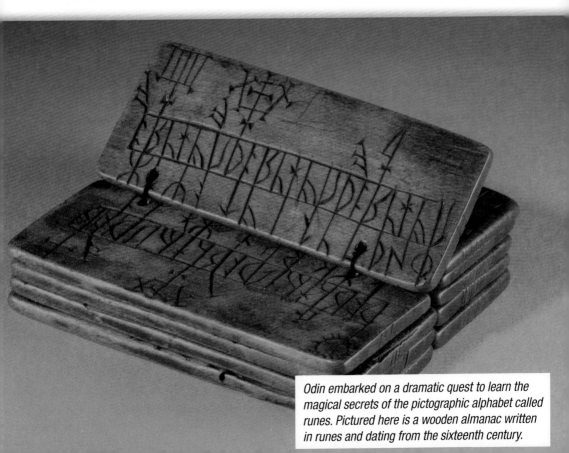

Odin embarked on a dramatic quest to learn the magical secrets of the pictographic alphabet called runes. Pictured here is a wooden almanac written in runes and dating from the sixteenth century.

The Missing Hammer

While Odin was sharing gifts with humanity, his son Thor was guarding gods and humans from threats. Thor relied on his magic hammer called Mjöllnir (meaning "Lightning") to fight the giants and other enemies of the gods and humans. When that powerful weapon was stolen, Thor went on a sometimes comic adventure to retrieve it.

As told in the *Poetic Edda*, one morning mighty Thor awakened from a deep sleep to find his reliable and beloved hammer, which he always kept beside his bed at night, missing. Determined to find the treasured object, he began to alert his fellow deities, hoping to enlist their aid. The first god Thor approached was the trickster Loki, who at that moment was residing in Asgard and claiming to help the Aesir. Loki agreed that the loss of Mjöllnir was extremely concerning because, if the giants found out, they might take advantage of the situation and attack Asgard.

Mjöllnir
Thor's mighty hammer

Thor and Loki talked it over, agreed that a giant must have stolen the hammer, and formed a plan to recover it. One vital element of the scheme consisted of Loki's traveling to Jotunheim—where the trickster was more welcome than the other Aesir—to see if he could figure out which giant was the guilty party. The two gods also concurred that if Loki went by horse, it would take too long. Therefore, Loki rushed to see the fertility goddess Freya and borrowed Valhamr, her magical cloak of feathers that allowed her to fly at high speeds through the sky.

Slipping into Valhamr, Loki soared over scores of rugged mountains and forested valleys until at last he caught sight of the tall, forbidding peaks of Jotunheim ahead. Swooping downward, he searched high and low until he found the estate of the king of the giants, Thrym. Loki was about to land near that monstrous being's enormous castle when he spied Thrym himself sitting on a big rock.

In this wood engraving, the Norse god of thunder, Thor, wields his mighty hammer as lightning strikes dramatically behind him.

Loki and Thrym had met on numerous occasions in the past, so the giant-king was aware of who the visitor was. Thrym gruffly asked what he wanted, and Loki got right to the point and asked if Thrym had stolen Thor's hammer. The giant surprised Loki by admitting it. Moreover, Thrym told him to go ahead and inform the gods and to add that there was only one way the object would ever be returned: Thor, Odin, and the other Aesir needed to agree to let Thrym marry the fantastically beautiful Freya.

The Wedding Plot

When Loki flew back to Asgard and told Thor and Freya about Thrym's ultimatum, they both became enraged. There was no way, Freya said, that she would ever marry a giant. Thor sympathized

The Original Story of the Hammer's Theft

The story of Thrym's theft of Thor's hammer and Thor's quest to retrieve it comes from an old Norse tale called "The Lay of Thrym," which dates to sometime in the 900s CE. This excerpt is from former University of Pittsburgh professor D.L. Ashliman's translation of the work. In it, Loki returns to Asgard after learning that Thrym stole the hammer, and Heimdall suggests that Thor should pretend to be Freya (or Freyja).

[Loki and Thor] hurried to Freyja's home, and Thor said: "Freyja, dress yourself in bridal linen! The two of us are going to the land of the giants." Freyja grew angry and foamed with rage. The entire hall shook with her fury. . . . She [refused to marry Thrym, so] all the gods and goddesses of the [Aesir] hurriedly assembled . . . to discuss how they might retrieve Thor's hammer. Heimdall, the fairest of the gods . . . foretold the future: "We shall dress Thor in bridal linen. . . . Let him wear a woman's clothes with a bundle of housewife's keys dangling about him and with bridal jewels at his breast and on his head."

D.L. Ashliman, trans., "Thrym's Lay," Furor Teutonics, July 14, 1999. www.furorteutonicus.eu.

and immediately called together a meeting of the Aesir. They agreed not only that no such marriage should happen but also that Thor should get his hammer back as soon as possible. Odin asked if anyone had a workable plan for retrieving the object. Heimdall, the guardian of Bifrost, said he did. His plan was for the gods to pretend to bless the marriage of Freya and Thrym. However, Heimdall called for Thor to disguise himself as Freya and present himself as Thrym's bride. When the time was right, Thor could snatch the hammer from the confused giant-king.

The manly Thor was not happy about dressing as a woman. But seeing no other way, he did so and traveled to Jotunheim. Thrym invited hundreds of his fellow giants to the wedding ceremony, which took place inside an immense cave. There was music, dancing, and plenty of food and wine. Thor, wearing a wig and hiding his beard behind a bridal veil, sat beside Thrym at the head table.

Before the ceremony commenced, Thrym announced that he had a special gift for his bride-to-be. He motioned to a servant, who carried in Thor's beloved hammer, and the ruler of the giants, who had been totally outwitted, placed the object right into the hands of the disguised Thor. Mere seconds later, the latter yanked off his disguise, called Thrym a low-life thief, and smashed the hammer into his head, crushing his skull. As the king's lifeless body fell to the floor, the other giants ran around in terrified confusion. That made it easy for Thor to use Mjöllnir to finish them all off.

When Odin and the other gods heard that the quest for the hammer had ended with the slaughter of the giants, they understood why Thor had taken that brutal step. The prevailing wisdom was that the gods stood for order and an organized universe, whereas the giants represented chaos and an end to social order. Moreover, prophecy held that in the far future the forces of chaos would try to destroy the gods and humanity. Hence, Thor was just doing what had to be done. As McCoy puts it, "When Thor smote the giants with the hammer, he was defending the cosmos and banishing the forces of chaos."[12] It was, however, a temporary reprieve, for the forces of chaos would return.

Warriors and Their Fates: The Compulsion to Fight

The fierce and proud Norse warrior Volund was also a skilled blacksmith and goldsmith. He was known for creating the finest iron, gold, and silver jewelry in the Viking lands. It was common for people from faraway towns to travel to his village to see him work and buy objects he had crafted.

One day, however, some of the those who visited Volund's forge had more nefarious intentions. Nidud, king of a distant Scandinavian realm, arrived with his queen and a contingent of armed soldiers. That monarch demanded that the renowned craftsman leave his village and come work at Nidud's palace. When Volund refused, the king decided to take him by force. But Nidud feared that a warrior of the smith's strength and fighting skills might be too hard to capture. So the king waited until Volund was having lunch and unarmed. Then Nidud signaled to his henchmen, who captured the burly blacksmith.

When the party of kidnappers returned to their kingdom and entered the palace, the queen noticed that Volund was mightily trying to break free. Fearfully, according to a surviving medieval version of the tale, she told her husband, "His teeth he shows [and] threatening are his eyes as a glistening serpent's. Let be severed his hamstrings and set him [on the remote island of] Sae-varstad."[13]

Nidud took his wife's advice and ordered that Volund's leg tendons be cut so that it would be difficult for him to run or fight; and the soldiers chained the warrior-craftsman on the nearby, tiny island, where his only visitor was the king himself. In the months that followed, Volund had no choice but to craft gold and silver trinkets for Nidud's luxurious abode.

However, the wicked ruler had not anticipated the extent of his captive's shrewdness and bravery. Volund used one of his black-smith tools to break his chains and swam from the island to the mainland. There, he killed a guard with his bare hands, took his sword, crept into the palace, and did some kidnapping of his own. Seizing the king's two sons, Volund slew them, made silver-lined goblets from their skulls, and sent the ghastly items to Nidud. After defeating many of the king's guards, the mighty warrior-craftsman donned a special winged cape he had fashioned and, to Nidud's amazement, soared away into the sky.

The Glorious Viking Death Cult

The valiant Volund flew not only into the sky but also into legend, becoming one of the select members of Norse mythology's company of memorable human heroes. Typically, those in that company were, like him, defiant, fearless, skilled in warfare, and more than willing to match cruelties directed at them with savagery of their own. They also did not overtly fear death, in part because they were certain that, as warriors, they would end up in Odin's army of heroes in the afterlife.

The fierce Norse warrior Volund was renowned for creating the finest iron, gold, and silver jewelry in the Viking world. His work would have resembled these Viking-era rings, bracelets, and necklaces.

Because the Norse were for centuries very devout believers in their gods and accepted most myths as real historical events, Viking warriors tended to strongly identify with the mythical heroes. That included a highly unusual mindset regarding death and the afterlife. Saint Louis University scholar Tom Shippey writes, "To put it bluntly, it's a kind of death cult."[14]

The members of that cult, Shippey continues, developed not only a psychological edge that allowed them to fight fearlessly but also at times a less-than-serious attitude toward dying. "The heroes of the Viking Age," he explains, "both gods and men, fixated as they seemed to be on death and defeat, *just did not seem able to take death and defeat seriously*." Often in the face of death, in battle or elsewhere, "they kept on making jokes, coming out with wisecracks." A large part of this strange attitude, Shippey suggests, came from the refusal of many Norse warriors to acknowledge defeat, "even in an impossible situation." Instead, "what was best was showing you could turn the tables, spoil your enemy's victory, make a joke out of death, [and] die laughing."[15]

For a great many Viking warriors, therefore, fearlessness was the highest virtue, the most moral trait an individual could possess. A stunning example consists of words said to have been spoken by the real and renowned Viking warrior-king Ragnar Lothbrok prior to his execution by an enemy. "The gods will invite me in," he stated. "In death there is no sighing. . . . The hours of life have passed [and] laughing shall I die."[16]

A Warrior's Death and the Afterlife

Ragnar's mention of the gods "inviting him in" is of course a reference to either Odin allowing him entrance into Valhalla or Freya welcoming him into Folkvangr. All Viking warriors expected, or at least ardently hoped, that they would end up in one of those mythical halls of the *einherjar*, or fallen heroes. The traditional belief was that when a warrior died on the battlefield, he might encounter a Valkyrie—one of the goddesses whose name means "choosers of the slain." It was a Valkyrie's duty to guide the einherjars' souls to the afterlife. Although either Valhalla or Folkvangr was an acceptable destination for most Norse warriors, Valhalla was much preferred, mainly because of Odin's exalted status as the All-Father.

Several myths describe Valhalla itself. Supposedly its walls were made of large spear shafts and the roof was covered by warriors' shields. Inside were benches and tables for feasting and lounging. Above the main door hung the carcass of a ferocious wolf, and a giant eagle flew around above it. In ancient northern European literature, those two animals often appeared as symbols of fighting or the battlefield.

einherjar
Warriors who died in battle and went to dwell with either Odin or Freya

Norse writers frequently mentioned the deaths of kings and other notable warriors in battle and how the divine forces prepared to receive them in the glorious afterlife. One surviving poem describes the death of the Norwegian monarch Eric Bloodaxe in 954. After attacking towns on the coasts of various

western European kingdoms, he ruled small sections of England and was slain in battle either there or in Scotland. The poet gives the following speech to Odin, who plans to welcome Eric and many of his dead soldiers into Valhalla. "What kind of dream is this," the All-Father asks, "that I had thought before daybreak I was preparing Valhalla for a slain army? I awakened the einherjar, asking them to get up to strew the benches and to rinse the drinking cups. I asked the Valkyries to bring [extra] wine, as if a leader should come."[17]

The Sword of Sigmund

In addition to known human heroes like Eric Bloodaxe, the Vikings often celebrated the several human heroes populating their collected myths. Although the myths about Odin, his sons

Thor and Baldr, and the war god Tyr were the most frequently cited tales about outstanding warriors, a handful of mythical human heroes constituted a close second in popularity. In fact, fully half of the huge *Poetic Edda* is devoted to the feats of legendary human warriors.

Of those accounts of the human heroes, by far the most famous and most often recited are those of the Volsungs. A family of celebrated warriors, their fortunes were repeatedly shaped by the interference and use of magic by the chief god, Odin. The first superhero, so to speak, of the Volsungs was Sigmund, son of the family namesake, Volsung, and his wife, Hljod. Sigmund had nine brothers. He also had a twin sister named Signy, with whom he was extremely close.

Volsungs

A mythical Norse family that was said to have produced several heroic warriors

The Warrior Cult's Extreme: The Berserkers

Most of the Norse warriors who glorified fighting in battle based on the exploits of the heroes of their myths were brave and fought hard. But a few in their ranks took the warrior mindset to an extreme, both physically and psychologically. They were known as the berserkers, who earned that name because they were said to go berserk on the battlefield. Devoting themselves totally to the chief god, Odin, whom they expected to personally meet in Valhalla, they fought in a kind of wild frenzy, supposedly channeling the spirit of creatures like bears and wolves. The Norse called this altered state of mind the *berserkergangr*, or "berserker's fury." Medieval eyewitness reports describe berserkers howling like wolves, biting the edges of their shields, and even foaming at the mouth. Some historians think these frantic fighters may have been under the influence of mind-altering herbs. And botanist Karsten Fatur agrees, singling out the henbane plant as the most likely culprit. The effects of ingesting it, he points out, "can range from agitation to full-blown rage . . . depending on the dosage and the individual's mental set." Although this cannot be proved for certain, he adds, henbane is an "appropriate theoretical intoxicant for the berserkers."

Quoted in Jennifer Ouellette, "Viking Berserkers May Have Used Henbane to Induce Trance-Like State," *Ars Technica*, September 18, 2019. https://arstechnica.com.

Sigmund's most famous tale revolves in large degree around the so-called Branstock Tree, a mighty oak that grew in the central courtyard of the Volsungs' mansion. It came to pass that the local king, Siggeir, arrived at the mansion one day and asked Volsung for the hand in marriage of his only daughter, Signy. The young woman reacted by calling Siggeir cruel and dishonest and refusing to marry him. But Volsung called her headstrong and sanctioned the marriage.

During the wedding celebration, an uninvited guest appeared. He was barefoot, had only one eye, and wore a blue cloak. Most in attendance were suspicious of him, and it turned out they had good reason to be. Suddenly, he yanked a large sword from his cloak and plunged the weapon into the trunk of the Branstock Tree. "Whoso draweth this sword from this stock, shall have the same as a gift from me, and shall find in good sooth that never bare he better sword in hand than is this."[18] The enigmatic figure then left the courtyard, and someone who followed him claimed that he seemed to vanish into thin air. At that point, many of those gathered speculated that the stranger had been Odin himself.

In the days that followed, many men, including Volsung, tried but failed to pull the sword from the tree. Finally, Sigmund gave it a try, and the weapon easily slipped from the oak and into his possession. Everyone was amazed. And King Siggeir, who assumed that magic was somehow involved, decided to get the weapon for himself. When Sigmund declined to sell it, the ruler flew into a rage and in the months that followed killed Volsung and all the Volsung children except for Sigmund and Signy. The brother and sister then joined forces and fought back. Employing the sword Odin had clearly intended for Sigmund's use, they slew Siggeir and his chief relatives and followers. Sigmund became king and years later died bravely in battle.

Sigurth and the Dragon

The common wisdom among the Norse regarding this myth was that Odin had selected Sigmund to rid the world of the evil Siggeir. And to ensure that would happen, the All-Father had intervened at the wedding and left behind a special weapon for the task. Later, Odin made sure that Sigmund died in battle. That way, no Viking doubted, Sigmund would, as a member of the warrior death cult, end up at Odin's side in Valhalla.

The prevailing belief, however, was that Sigmund's equally famous son, Prince Sigurth, did not make it into Valhalla. Instead, Sigurth's soul went to Helheim and there, presumably, lived on

Twins Signy and Sigmund (pictured) were members of the celebrated (and real) Volsung family of Norse warriors. The fortunes of the family were said to have been influenced by Odin's magic.

as an average Norse male of no consequence. In other words, although Sigurth did not suffer in the afterlife, he was denied the great reward and glory of feasting at Odin's table in Valhalla.

This fact may at first appear strange, considering that in life Sigurth did make quite a name for himself as a hero. Indeed, he gained widespread fame for his exploits as a dragon slayer. When Sigurth reached his early twenties, his royal tutor, Regin, suggested that he try to acquire a fabulous treasure trove con- trolled by a fearsome dragon. Regin knew a great deal about this dragon because it happened to be his own brother, Fafnir. After stealing the treasure, Fafnir had purposely exposed himself to a curse that had transformed him into an immense dragon, which now jealously guarded the treasure in some nearby hills.

Sigurth traveled into those hills and managed to slay Fafnir. Al- though a heroic feat, to be sure, it alone did not ensure the young man's eventual entrance into Valhalla. This is because a crucial aspect of the Norse warrior death cult was that the fighter had to

To Enter the Afterlife: Viking Funerals

One famed aspect of the Norse warrior death cult that has been depicted in novels and movies is the Viking's funeral, which honored a warrior's death on the battlefield and enabled his entrance into the afterlife. One eyewitness account of such colorful ceremonies was penned in 922 by the Muslim traveler Ibn Fadlan. About the funeral of a Viking chief on a Baltic Sea beach, he said that someone killed a slave girl and placed her body near that of the chief in the center of a Viking ship. Then a naked mourner

took hold of a piece of wood and set fire to it. He walked backwards . . . with the lighted piece of wood in one hand and the other hand on his anus. . . . He ignited the wood that had been set up under the ship [and] then the people came forward with sticks and firewood. . . . The wood caught fire, and then the ship, the pavilion, the man, the slave-girl and all it contained. A dreadful wind arose and the flames leapt higher and blazed fiercely.

Quoted in Mark Miller, "The 10th Century Chronicle of the Violent, Orgiastic Funeral of a Viking Chieftain," *History, Archaeology, Folklore and So On* (blog), April 25, 2015. https://historyandsoon.wordpress.com.

die in battle, with a sword or other weapon in hand. Odin hoped that Sigurth would eventually die that way.

Instead, Sigurth allowed himself to be drawn into a complex web of impulsive, dishonorable love affairs. As a result, a woman who felt betrayed by him had him murdered while he was asleep in bed. "Because this greatest of heroes died in bed and not in battle," University of Colorado scholar Jackson Crawford explains, "Sigurth [was] denied to Odin and his hall of dead heroes, Valhalla. Odin groomed Sigmund and got him for his army. But he groomed his son Sigurth and lost him."[19]

The contrast between the fates of two heroes—Sigmund and his son Sigurth—illustrates the restrictive demands of the cult that compelled Norse warriors to seek out and fight battles. The set of beliefs contained in this odd and unique cultural mindset recognized that there were only two kinds of death—bad and good. "The choice isn't between living and dying," Crawford points out. "It's between dying badly and dying well on the day that you're going to die anyway."[20] Put simply, Sigmund died well. But his son died badly, and that was why their souls ended up in very different places.

Giants, Dwarfs, and Other Strange Creatures

One of the more popular stories from the *Poetic Edda* is that of the dwarf Alvis, who loved to collect and recite facts about the World Tree and the many races and beings who dwelled there. Indeed, eventually Alvis became known far and wide as the most learned of all the dwarfs. One problem with that fame was that he let it go to his head and fancied himself more worthy and important than he was.

Eventually, the self-centered Alvis made a grave mistake. He came to believe that his amassed knowledge made him equal to the Aesir. "My place is in Asgard, among the gods," he told several of his dwarf friends. "Only they can understand my wisdom and make everyone pay tribute to me."[21] Then he told them that he had set his sights on wooing and marrying Thrud, the daughter of the mighty thunder deity, Thor.

Hearing this, the other dwarfs became worried about Alvis. They reminded him of the scary reality that any dwarf who left the dark realm of the dwarfs, Nidavellir, and was struck by sunlight would turn to stone. Alvis retorted that of course he was aware of that fact. Prudently, he had decided to travel to Asgard at night, when the sun was not in the sky. "And then," he added, "I can marry a goddess, and then the Aesir will have to admit me to Asgard."[22]

Following this plan, Alvis waited until the sun set and made his way to the border of Asgard. There he encountered none other than Thor himself. "I've come to claim Thrud, my bride," the delusional dwarf told the tall, muscular god standing before him. "I can't wait for my wedding night, and I don't mean to hang around here any longer than I have to."[23]

Although Alvis was indeed very knowledgeable, at that moment he had no clue how much trouble he was in, for Thor had no intention of allowing his daughter to wed a dwarf. After all, from the Aesir's viewpoint, the inhabitants of Nidavellir were far inferior to the residents of Asgard. With that in mind, Thor began asking Alvis simple questions, and the dwarf, wanting to show off his collected knowledge, kept answering them, one after another. This went on for the rest of the night until the sun's golden disk rose from behind a distant peak. At the last second, Alvis realized the danger, but it was too late. In an instant he congealed into a block of stone.

Dwarfs and Elves

Alvis's unfortunate fate was a reminder that the mythical Norse race that spawned him—the dwarfs, sometimes referred to as the "dark elves"—were almost always confined to their underground kingdom of Nidavellir. Short, stocky, often bearded beings, the Norse dwarfs closely resembled the dwarfs of German mythology. And because the latter inspired famed novelist J.R.R. Tolkien, the dwarfs in his epic *Lord of the Rings* trilogy are in a sense cousins of the Norse dwarfs.

According to the Norse myths, the dwarfs began as worms crawling from the corpse of Ymir, the first Norse giant. In time those creatures grew heads and limbs and gained intelligence and various talents. In their subterranean realm of Nidavellir,

sometimes called Svartalfheim, they mined gold and other minerals and forged iron and other metals in hundreds of forges. Eventually, they became skilled enough to craft not only beautiful jewelry and sturdy swords but also Thor's hammer and Odin's spear.

Besides the dwarfs, the World Tree was home to numerous other kinds of nondivine and nonhuman races and creatures. Among them were the residents of an aboveground kingdom known as Alfheim, or "Elf-Land." The principal Norse elves, the Ljosalfar, or "Light Elves," looked like humans, only taller and, without exception, more attractive. Medieval Norse writings frequently describe the elves as noble-looking and ethereal, or angel-like. Some legends claimed that the Ljosalfar may have initially been an offshoot of the secondary race of gods—the Vanir. That would explain why some elves were said to be able to perform magical feats, such as healing incurable diseases.

Some elves interacted with people, while others avoided contact with humans. In Daniel McCoy's words, in the Norse writings the residents of Alfheim have a mix of varied contacts and "relations with humans. Elves commonly cause human illnesses, but they also have the power to heal them, and seem especially willing to do so if sacrifices are offered to them. Humans and elves can interbreed and produce half-human, half-elfin children, who often have the appearance of humans but possess extraordinary intuitive and magical powers."[24]

Some elves were also known to protect ordinary human children, as in the popular myth of an elf named Andrias. In that story, when a child carved an animal from wood and left it on a bedroom windowsill, Andrias would accept the gift and thereafter keep the youngster safe. The elf might also leave the child at treat in the carving's place.

Zombies, Sprites, and More

The Norse myths also contain references to zombies known as the Draugar. Most often they were evil or greedy people in life, whose punishment after death was to eat human flesh and drink human blood. Supposedly, these decaying creatures had superhuman strength and the ability to grow larger or smaller at will. Like the dragon Fafnir, the Draugar felt compelled to hoard gold and other treasures. For that reason, they tended to hang out in their graves to protect any valuables that were buried with them.

Nevertheless, Norse zombies occasionally left their graves and roamed around human villages hoping to scare and devour the residents or the local livestock. In one well-known Norse zombie

A Helpful Troll

Among the many strange beings inhabiting the Norse myths were trolls, of which there were two types. The first consisted of big, very ugly ones that lived in forests and mountains; the second type of troll was quite small, gnomelike, and inhabited caves or underground burrows. Both kinds of trolls were said to be dim-witted. Although some could be mean-spirited or mischievous, others were sometimes helpful or even kind to humans. An example of a helpful troll appears in the myth of a farmer's son named Askeladden, whose two brothers had gone into the woods to gather firewood but had returned early, saying they had seen a troll and in fear had run home. Less timid than his siblings, Askeladden entered the forest, taking with him a piece of cheese. When he came upon the troll, the boy held up the cheese, telling the creature that it was really a rock. When Askeladden crumbled the cheese in his hand, the not-so-bright troll figured the young man must be fantastically strong to be able to crush a rock. So the creature tried to get on the boy's good side. Thereafter, the troll helped Askeladden gather wood and did several other favors for him.

myth, a disreputable man named Thorolf became one of the Draugar after he died. As he decayed, his body swelled until it was as big as that of an ox. Moreover, it smelled so rank that any birds and other animals that came near his grave, near the Icelandic village of Hvammur, first went mad and then dropped dead. It was common knowledge among the Norse that the only ways to kill a Draugar were to either burn or dismember it.

Other strange creatures populating the Norse World Tree included Fossegrimens, which were sprites or fairies that lived in lakes and streams and at times demanded tolls from passing travelers. Large bodies of water were also home to krakens, enormous squid-like sea monsters that sank human ships. In the forests, huldras, shaped like women but having long cows' tails, kidnapped men and kept them prisoner. These creatures were often the antagonists in Norse heroic tales.

kraken

A huge squid-like sea monster

Huge Serpentine Beasts

At times, the dwarfs, elves, zombies, and other diverse cave, forest, and water creatures in the Norse myths were overshadowed by two kinds of beings who shared the World Tree with the gods and humans. First, there were the dragons. These huge, serpentine beasts were popular motifs in Viking culture. Perhaps the most famous example was the use of carved dragons' heads on the fronts and backs of Viking warships. The general belief was that those sculpted images stood for qualities like strength and courage. In addition, battlefield flags and various artworks featuring dragons were common throughout the Norse lands.

Viking warships such as the ones depicted in this painting, often featured carvings of dragon heads at the front and rear of the vessels. The carvings symbolized strength and courage.

Still Another Norse Monster

Out of the huge menagerie of nonhuman creatures that lived in the Norse World Tree, dragons, krakens, zombies, and some of the more mean-spirited giants can all be thought of as monsters. Another bizarre species in that unsavory group was that of the mara (or mare). The maras were disembodied demons or witches that sat on people's chests at night, causing them to experience terrible nightmares. In fact, the word *nightmare* itself literally combines the word *night* with the name of the demon-like mare. The Norse (along with several other peoples of northern and eastern Europe) believed that witches and demons were not the only types of maras. Others were supposedly the spirits of ordinary people, especially children and teenagers, who wandered from house to house and bed to bed while they themselves remained asleep in their own beds. In one of Odin's myths, he worried that because his spirit frequently made mara-like journeys on dark, quiet nights, his soul might one day fail to return to his body.

To a large extent, the Vikings' images of dragons were based on stories from mythology. In addition to the widely popular tale of the slaying of the treasure-guarding Fafnir by the Volsung hero Sigurth, almost as famous was the story of the dragon killer Frotho. More properly known as King Frotho I, he was an early Danish ruler whom modern historians consider fictitious. Supposedly, he traveled from Denmark to a distant island in the Baltic Sea, where a fierce dragon dwelled in a cave. That creature was not only big and immensely strong but also possessed poisonous saliva, which it spit at any humans who came too close. To keep the poison from touching his skin, the story goes, Frotho carried a specially made cowhide shield. After stabbing the creature to death, he returned to Denmark in triumph.

Ferocious and scary as they were, Fafnir and the Baltic Sea dragon paled in comparison to the largest, most dangerous of all the Norse dragons—the Midgard Serpent. It was also called the Girdle of Earth and the World Serpent. This is because it was so huge that its body wound all the way around the World Tree. As H.R.E. Davidson points out, this dragon was the symbolic ancestor of all the dragons in the myths of northern Europe. "Beside him," Davidson wrote, "we must set the fiery dragons of northern mythology, emerging from the depths of the earth, from rocks, caves, or burial mounds of the dead."[25]

The Norse had a popular myth that explained where the World Serpent came from. According to that tale, the shape-shifting god Loki met and mated with a female giant named Angrboda, who then gave birth to a baby dragon. In the months that followed, it grew larger and larger, especially its tail, which soon measured several miles in length.

Not surprisingly, the other gods viewed this hideous child in their midst with disgust and apprehension. And Odin took it upon himself to get rid of it. Seizing the creature, he hurled it into the enormous sea that encircled the World Tree, likely hoping the beast would drown there. But Loki's awful offspring did not perish in the depths. Instead, it remained under the waves, and grew longer and longer until it encircled the world.

Attacks by the Jotnar

The other important nondivine, nonhuman beings in the Norse myths were the giants. It must be emphasized that the Norse giants—the Jotnar—were not all huge, towering creatures. Although some Jotnar were true giants, as Norse cultural historian Jess Scott explains, "many of them [were] the same size as humans." In Norse lore, therefore, the term *giant* is most often "used as the name of a group of beings, rather than as a reference to any physical trait."[26]

The Jotnar inhabited numerous environments in and around the World Tree, from snow-covered mountains to underground caverns to forests and even to the sea's depths. The giants also had varied feelings about the gods and humans. Some Jotnar were friendly toward and even intermarried with the gods; for example, Thor's mother was a giant, and so was Loki's father. However, another very powerful and dangerous group of giants hated the gods and humans and wanted to annihilate them.

In fact, occasionally members of that menacing group of Jotnar brazenly launched attacks on Asgard, hoping to defeat the Aesir. One of the better-known Norse tales dealing with such assaults involved the biggest giant of them all—Hrungnir. Not only was he some seven times taller than Odin (whose height was seven feet, or 213 cm), that giant's head and heart were composed of stone, which made him quite difficult to wound or kill.

Thor wields his powerful hammer against Hrungnir, a member of the race of giants known as the Jotnar. Hrungnir's attack on Asgard failed thanks to Thor's quick response.

Despite these advantages, Hrungnir knew that attacking Asgard would not be easy. If Thor were there, the giant reasoned, there was no sense in even trying because that god's famous hammer was too formidable. It could shatter even the solid stone of Hrungnir's head and heart.

Therefore, this biggest of the Jotnar waited until he heard that Thor would be away for a while and then initiated his assault on the gods' abode. Making it across the rainbow bridge, Bifrost, Hrungnir burst into Asgard's main palace. There, he insulted the gods, calling them puny and powerless, and threatened to crush them all, except for Thor's wife, Sif. The interloper said he would make her his slave. Reacting to this tirade, Odin and the other gods quickly crowded around Sif to protect her and prepared to fight.

At that very moment, however, mighty Thor unexpectedly appeared on the scene. Grasping his renowned lethal hammer, in an instant he took a stance between the giant and the assembled deities. The expression on Hrungnir's face suddenly changed from smugness to abject fear. He considered running away but realized it was too late, and in desperation, he threw his only weapon—a millstone—at Thor. As Davidson tells it, Thor countered by hurling his hammer and "the weapons met in mid-air." The hammer easily shattered the millstone and "went on to strike Hrungnir's skull and break it in pieces."[27]

Thor had saved Asgard and his fellow divinities, and not for the first time. But would the gods always manage to fend off attacks by the giants and other mortal enemies? Unfortunately, a prophecy by the Norns claimed that the days of the Aesir, and of their human allies too, were numbered. Making matters worse, the prediction said their destroyers would be the children of Loki, who would betray them. The Aesir wondered whether the prophecy could be avoided. And if so, perhaps it would be best to deal with the disloyal Loki first. Though the gods did not fear their end, they did not simply accept their fate when their combined power was formidable.

CHAPTER 5

Loki and His Children: The Fall of the Gods

The trickster god, Loki, had originally earned that nickname by being mischievous and at times somewhat defiant and disobedient in his relationships with the other gods. But eventually, the Norns, the strange female beings who could see into the future, predicted that Loki would turn on his fellow deities and bring about their doom. He would, they said, lead a pack of his own monstrous offspring, along with other dastardly allies, in an all-out war against the gods and humans.

Because signs of their impending fate did not immediately come to pass, the gods lived with this knowledge for ages. However, Odin, Thor, and the other Aesir naturally wanted to avoid that disastrous future if they could, so they eventually gathered and decided there was no other choice but to capture and imprison Loki. Since he was the ringleader of the rebellion in the Norns' prophecy, keeping him under lock and key seemed the logical way to forestall the prophecy.

When Loki heard that the other deities were after him, he fled Asgard and hid near the top of a distant mountain. There, he constructed a house with four open doors so that at night he could keep an eye out for his pursuers in all four directions. In the daytime, meanwhile, he assumed the form of a salmon and hid beneath a nearby waterfall. This ruse failed, however, in part because Loki was not nearly as smart as Odin, who figured out the trick. Once discovered, the Loki salmon leaped into the air to escape, but Thor caught him.

A Danish oil painting depicts the three Norns. According to Norse mythology, these enigmatic female entities both create and control fate.

Forced to change back into his normal form, Loki was taken to a cave near Asgard and there bound with chains. Directly above his head the gods placed a poisonous snake, which dripped powerful venom onto his face. It was so caustic that from time to time it made him shake violently, which set off earthquakes felt by

This illustration portrays Loki's agonizing punishment. The Norse trickster god, bound and defenseless, looks up in fear as a venomous snake drips poison onto his face.

the humans who dwelled in nearby Midgard. Day after day, year after year, and decade after decade, the trickster suffered this way, while constantly thinking about the Norns' prophecy and anxiously waiting to break free and get his revenge.

The Foretelling of Ragnarok

Loki had good reason to hope that he would eventually gain his freedom and prevail. This was because of the amazing reliability of the Norns. In all the countless years of the world's existence, they had never lied; nor had their predictions ever been wrong. And Loki, Odin, and the other gods were aware of that fact. They listened grimly when the prophecy warned that there would come a climactic, enormous battle called Ragnarok, which translates roughly as the "Twilight of the Gods." In that fearsome encounter, the Aesir and their allies, the humans, would struggle against the forces of chaos, evil, and anarchy, but ultimately lose the battle.

Despite knowing for centuries that their eventual destruction was assured, both the residents of Asgard and the humans refused either to surrender or to lose hope. In an incredible display of heroism and positive thinking, they resolved to fight on with their last ounce of strength. As mythologist Edith Hamilton writes, over Asgard, stronghold of the Norse gods,

> hangs the threat of an inevitable doom. The gods know that a day will come when they will be destroyed [and] Asgard will fall in ruins. The cause the forces of good are fighting to defend against the forces of evil is hopeless. Nevertheless, the gods will fight for it to the end. Necessarily, the same is true of humanity. . . . They know that they cannot save themselves, not by any courage or endurance or great deed. Even so, they [will] not yield. They [will] die resisting.[28]

Sitting solemnly on his throne in Asgard, Odin periodically contemplated the prophecy and the part he and his fellow deities were to play in it. That this was so often on his mind partly explains why he was frequently such a sad and gloomy figure. He was aware of the bleak future awaiting the gods and humanity and anguished over it. His preoccupation with that depressing knowledge also explains why he so often sought more wisdom. It is likely that in the hidden corners of his vast intellect lurked an earnest hope that he would stumble upon some shred of information that might alter that ill-fated future.

If there were some sliver of hope that the Norns could be wrong, the All-Father asked himself, what could the gods do to help make such a brighter future a reality? The most reasonable answer he could conjure up was in the very wording of the prophecy itself. It stated that Loki and his most monstrous offspring would lead the insurrection against the Aesir. Logically, therefore, Loki must first be kept securely bound—forever if need be.

Second, it made sense for the gods to go after Loki's evil progeny, one by one, and either kill or incapacitate them. One of those monstrous children was the gigantic Midgard Serpent, which Loki had named Jormungand. There was also Hel, the hideous hag who ruled the underworld, and a huge and vicious wolf named Fenrir, which had razor-sharp teeth and smelled like rotting flesh.

Picturing those three dangerous beings in his mind, Odin realized that he had already tried to rid the world of Jormungand by drowning it. But that attempt had failed, and now the great serpent was bigger than ever. As for Hel, Odin told himself, she was extremely strong and possessed potent magical powers; moreover, she had made her subterranean kingdom so self-contained and impregnable that even Odin himself would find it difficult to enter it and dislodge her.

Chaining the Great Wolf

That left the third and most destructive and frightening of Loki's repulsive brood—the giant wolf Fenrir. It was important to deal with

How the Gods and Monsters Fell

The final battle of Ragnarok is described in considerable detail in the *Prose Edda*. The following excerpt, which foretells which god will fight which monster, constitutes only a small part of the section about the fall of the gods.

> Then shall Heimdall rise up and blow mightily in the Gjallar-Horn, and awaken all the gods; and they shall hold council together. . . . Then shall the [Aesir] put on their war-weeds, and all the champions, and advance to the field [of battle]. Odin rides first with the gold helmet [and] his spear, which is called Gungnir. He shall go forth against [the giant wolf] Fenrir; and Thor . . . shall have his hands full to fight against the Midgard Serpent. Freyr shall contend with [the giant] Surtr, and a hard encounter shall there be between them before Freyr falls. . . . Then shall the [monstrous] dog Garmr be loosed [and] he shall do battle with Tyr, and each become the other's slayer. Thor shall put to death the Midgard Serpent, and shall stride away nine paces from that spot; then shall he fall dead to the earth.

Arthur G. Brodeur, trans., *The Prose Edda*. New York: American-Scandinavian Foundation, 1916, p. 79.

the creature because the consensus among the gods was that it would likely be the first monster to attack Asgard. After thinking on the matter, Odin decided that the best approach would be to confine the massive creature somewhere within Asgard. That way, the gods could keep a close eye on it until they could figure out a way to kill it.

To that end, the All-Father told a group of gods to hunt down Fenrir, wait until it was asleep, and then stealthily bind it. For that formidable task, Odin had his blacksmiths forge a large, strong iron collar and chain. The first part of the plan went well, as the hunters found the wolf and succeeded in applying the collar and chain before it awakened. The problem was that when Fenrir did wake up, it easily snapped the chain. The gods tried a second, stronger chain, but it too was not strong enough to hold the wolf.

At this point, Odin realized that ordinary chains, no matter how thick, were useless for the task at hand. Delving deep into his vast store of collected knowledge, he remembered the special talents of a particular tribe of dwarfs. The leader of the Aesir ordered a servant named Skirnir to ride at top speed to those underground crafters and offer them wagonloads of treasure in exchange for creating a fetter that would bind Fenrir.

Only a few days later, Skirnir returned with what he said was the strongest chain in the world, despite it being so thin it was almost invisible. The dwarfs had named it Gleipnir. According to the *Prose Edda*, "It was made of six things: the noise a cat makes

Loki's giant wolf Fenrir (pictured) fights back against a group of Norse gods who were ordered by Odin to entrap the beast.

in foot-fall, the beard of a woman, the roots of a rock, the sinews of a bear, the breath of a fish, and the spittle of a bird." This time when the gods attempted to bind the wolf, they succeeded. When Fenrir "lashed out, the fetter became hardened; and the more he struggled against it, the tighter the band was."[29]

Odin and the other deities rejoiced at their success in gaining control of the giant wolf. The only member of the Aesir without a smile on his face was the war god Tyr, for the beast had bitten off one of his hands during the struggle to bind it. To his credit, Tyr took the injury in stride, commenting that it was a small price to pay for keeping a murderous monster from running amok.

The Doomsday Battle

Despite their best hopes and efforts, the gods eventually had to accept that the Norns' prophecy of Ragnarok was inevitable. This became obvious when certain ominous signs of the coming apocalypse finally came to pass. First, there came Fimbulvetr, a freakishly long and abnormally cold winter during which most crops died and thousands of humans starved to death. Then three red roosters crowed so loud that they could be heard for hundreds of miles. One rooster warned the giants of the coming battle, the second warned the humans, and the third warned the gods. Next, Heimdall, divine protector of the rainbow bridge, produced a blast on his trumpet that signaled to the dead souls in Valhalla, informing them to prepare for the doomsday battle.

Solemnly, the gods, followed by their human allies, marched out to meet the enemy. As they did so, the surrounding seas foamed and swirled, and huge waves pounded the shore, all caused by the dragon Jormungand as it lifted its miles-long hulk onto the land to join in the battle. Meanwhile, in his cave prison, Loki finally broke his bonds, and he hurried as fast as he could to take charge of the forces of chaos and evil. Also, fearsome Fenrir broke free from Gleipnir, and

Fimbulvetr

An unusually long and bitter winter that directly preceded Ragnarok

How Many, Though Not All, Norse Myths Faded

For the most part, many of the old Norse myths were eventually forgotten or else ignored by most Vikings. The chief cause was the adoption of Christianity by the vast majority of Norse during the 1100s and 1200s. The Christian religion presented believers with a far more positive and hopeful view of the future than the traditional myths did—in particular, the fatalistic tale of Ragnarok that foretold the end of gods and humans. Much more appealing was the Christian concept that believers would be rewarded with eternal life in a peaceful heaven. Still, some Vikings, along with the first several generations of their descendants, kept some of the old myths alive, partly out of nostalgia for the world of their ancestors and partly for entertainment value, since, like all myths, those stories were fun to tell or listen to. During this cultural transition, some older Norse mythical ideas were incorporated into Christian beliefs and rituals. For example, some people associated the Christian cross with Thor's famous hammer, Mjöllnir, and wore jewelry depicting both at the same time.

many of the giants followed that monstrous wolf toward the fateful final fight.

As the forces of good and evil converged on each other on that terrible day, the ground heaved like ocean waves and the stars disappeared from the sky, leaving behind a scary black void. Along the tremendous, kingdom-sized branches of the World Tree, mountains shook. And some crumbled, forming towering landslides that smashed into cities, towns, and villages, killing untold numbers of people, animals, and creatures, good and bad alike.

Blood was spilled on a massive scale as the valiant Aesir struggled with every fiber of their beings to reverse the inevitable. And because, as the Norns had known, such a feat is impossible, one by one they met noble ends. "Odin and the champions of men [fought] more valiantly than anyone [had] ever fought before," Daniel McCoy writes. "But it [was not] enough."[30] The leader of the gods was swallowed by Fenrir, and the other deities were defeated in their own titanic combats. Then the great World Tree shuddered and fell into hapless ruin as the surviving giants and monsters, wounded and miserable, crawled through its broken branches.

After the End?

Religiously and mythologically speaking, the Norse were almost unique among the peoples of the past in envisioning the ultimate fall of their gods in a horrifying end-time. However, not all the Vikings could bring themselves to be so fatalistic. Although the devastation of Ragnarok weighed upon many Norse, some alternative versions of the story developed over time. In one, although most of the gods and humans perished, a few survived the catastrophe and slowly but steadily rebuilt the world over the course of centuries. Another similar myth claimed that all the gods did die, but two humans lived—a man named Lif and his wife, Lofthrasir. And they and their offspring repopulated the world.

No matter which of the doomsday myths various Vikings accepted, one point they could all agree on was that their cherished traditional gods had been supremely brave and honorable figures that everyone could admire. And that is the core of the enlightening and powerful lesson that emerges from Norse mythology for people everywhere. As H.R.E. Davidson so beautifully phrased it:

Lif and Lofthrasir

Two humans who survive doomsday in an alternative version of the bleak tale of Ragnarok

The picture of human qualities that emerges from the Norse myths is a noble one. The gods are heroic figures, humans writ large, who led dangerous, individualistic lives, yet at the same time . . . [possessed] a firm sense of values. . . . They would rather give up their lives than surrender those values [and] they would fight on as long as they could, since life was well worth it. . . . We find in these myths [a] spirit of heroic resignation. Humanity is born to trouble, but courage, adventure, and the wonders of life are matters for thankfulness, to be enjoyed while life is still granted to us.[31]

SOURCE NOTES

Introduction: Eager Achievers in an Enchanted World

1. William R. Short, "Supernatural Beings in Norse Society," Hurstwic. www.hurstwic.org.
2. Daniel McCoy, "Velkomin. Welcome," Norse Mythology for Smart People. https://norse-mythology.org.
3. Quoted in Daniel McCoy, "The Vikings' Selfish Individualism," Norse Mythology for Smart People. https://norse-mythology.org.

Chapter 1: A Tree So Vast: The Mythical Norse World

4. Quoted in Benjamin Thorpe, trans., *The Elder Edda*. London: Norroena Society, 1907, p. 1.
5. Magnus Magnusson, *Hammer of the North: Myths and Heroes of the Viking Age*. New York: Putnam, 1986, p. 49.
6. Daniel McCoy, "Hel (the Underworld)," Norse Mythology for Smart People. https://norse-mythology.org.
7. H.R.E. Davidson, *Scandinavian Mythology*. New York: Peter Bedrick, 1986, pp. 59–60.
8. Beth Daley, "Norse Gods Make a Comeback Thanks to Neil Gaiman. Here's Why Their Appeal Endures," The Conversation, February 21, 2017. https://theconversation.com.

Chapter 2: Thor's Hammer and Odin's Wisdom: Divine Quests

9. Davidson, *Scandinavian Mythology*, p. 213.
10. Davidson, *Scandinavian Mythology*, p. 213.
11. Daniel McCoy, "Odin's Discovery of the Runes," Norse Mythology for Smart People. https://norse-mythology.org.
12. Daniel McCoy, "Thor's Hammer," Norse Mythology for Smart People. https://norse-mythology.org.

Chapter 3: Warriors and Their Fates: The Compulsion to Fight

13. Quoted in Benjamin Thorpe, trans., *The Elder Eddas of Saemund Sigfusson*. London: Norroena Society, 1906, pp. 123–24.
14. Tom Shippey, *Laughing Shall I Die: Lives and Deaths of the Great Vikings*. London: Reaction, 2018, p. 14.
15. Shippey, *Laughing Shall I Die*, p. 26.
16. Quoted in Shippey, *Laughing Shall I Die*, p. 87.
17. Quoted in Noah Tetzner, "Valhalla: How Viking Belief in a Glorious Afterlife Empowered Warriors," History.com, March 3, 2021. www.history.com.
18. Quoted in William Morris and Eirikr Magnusson, trans., "From the Volsung Saga," Maricopa Community Colleges. https://open.maricopa.edu.
19. Jackson Crawford, "The Fall of Sigurth, the Great Volsung Hero," Wondrium Daily, August 3, 2022. ww.wondriumdaily.com.
20. Quoted in Tetzner, "Valhalla."

Chapter 4: Giants, Dwarfs, and Other Strange Creatures

21. Quoted in Angus Sutherland, "Dwarf Alvis ('All-Wise') Who Was Tricked by God Thor and Turned into Stone," Ancient Pages, May 27, 2019. www.ancientpages.com.
22. Quoted in Sutherland, "Dwarf Alvis ('All-Wise') Who Was Tricked by God Thor and Turned into Stone."
23. Quoted in Sutherland, "Dwarf Alvis ('All-Wise') Who Was Tricked by God Thor and Turned into Stone."
24. Daniel McCoy, "Elves," Norse Mythology for Smart People. https://norse-mythology.org.
25. Davidson, *Scandinavian Mythology*, p. 138.
26. Jess Scott, "Who Are the Jotnar in Norse Mythology?," Life in Norway, October 8, 2021. www.lifeinnorway.net.
27. Davidson, *Scandinavian Mythology*, p. 41.

Chapter 5: Loki and His Children: The Fall of the Gods

28. Edith Hamilton, *Mythology*. New York: Grand Central, 1999, p. 300.
29. Arthur G. Brodeur, trans., *The Prose Edda*. New York: American-Scandinavian Foundation, 1916, pp. 43, 45.
30. Daniel McCoy, "Ragnarok," Norse Mythology for Smart People. https://norse-mythology.org.
31. Davidson, *Scandinavian Mythology*, p. 218.

Books

Padraic Colum, *Loki: The Mischief Behind the Legend*. Monument, CO: Wordfire, 2022.

Neil Gaiman, *Norse Mythology*. 3 vols. Milwaukie, OR: Dark Horse, 2021.

Neil M. Hamilton, *Norse Mythology*. Independently published, 2019.

Gunnar Hylnsson, *Norse Myths, Paganism, Magic, Vikings, and Runes*. Independently published, 2022.

Henry Romano, *Myths and Legends of the Norse*. London: DTTY, 2022.

Isabel Wyatt, *Norse Myths and Viking Legends*. Edinburgh, Scotland: Floris, 2020.

Internet Sources

Joshua J. Mark, "Ten Norse Mythology Facts You Need to Know," World History Encyclopedia, September 21, 2021. www.world history.org.

Dattatreya Manadal, "The Most Powerful Norse Gods and Goddesses," Realm of History, January 29, 2018. www.realmof history.com.

Daniel McCoy, "The Enchanted World," Norse Mythology for Smart People. https://norse-mythology.org.

Andrew McKay, "Creatures in Norse Mythology," Life in Norway, July 19, 2018. www.lifeinnorway.net.

David Nikel, "Viking Religion: From the Norse Gods to Christianity," Life in Norway, August 21, 2019. www.lifeinnorway.net.

Mark Oliver, "8 Norse Gods with Stories You'll Never Learn in School," All That's Interesting, December 15, 2021. https://allthatsinteresting.com.

Ansel Pereira, "100 Most Powerful Gods and Goddesses of War," Owlcation, June 15, 2021. https://owlcation.com.

Jess Scott, "A Beginner's Guide to Norse Mythology," Life in Norway, December 3, 2020. www.lifeinnorway.net.

Sons of the Vikings, "Viking Lore: A Quick Intro to Norse Eddas and Sagas," July 3, 2020. https://sonsofvikings.com.

Swedish History Museum, "The Mythological World of the Vikings." https://historiska.se.

Swedish History Museum, "Odin: The One-Eyed Father." https://historiska.se.

Koen Uffing, "Four Forgotten Gods of Norse Mythology," Medium, July 15, 2020. https://medium.com.

Websites

The Field Museum
https://www.fieldmuseum.org/discover/on-exhibit/vikings
The website of this renowned museum in Chicago, Illinois, features all kinds of information about the Viking Age, including Norse religious beliefs, myths, and rituals; voyages and exploration; and daily life.

Museum of Ventura County
https://venturamuseum.org/virtual-exhibits/nordic-myths-and-legends-george-stuart-historical-figures
This Southern California museum has a prominent section on the Norse peoples and their gods. The website features four informative documentaries about various aspects of Viking life and lore. The site also includes a section on the work of noted historian and artist George Stuart, who created large, three-dimensional figures of the Norse gods.

Norse Mythology for Smart People
https://norse-mythology.org
Written by David McCoy, a noted scholar of Norse myths and folklore, this site contains a rounded, detailed look at the Norse myths, with numerous links to supportive articles, including ones on the various Norse gods, Norse cosmology, Viking culture, and diverse Norse writings.

INDEX